Temperate Forests

PETER BENOIT

Children's Press®
An Imprint of Scholastic Inc.
New York Toronto London Auckland Sydney
Mexico City New Delhi Hong Kong
Danbury, Connecticut

Content Consultant
Thomas Pypker, PhD
Michigan Technological University
Houghton, Michigan

Library of Congress Cataloging-in-Publication Data

Benoit, Peter, 1955–
 Temperate forests / Peter Benoit.
    p. cm.—(A true book)
 Includes bibliographical references and index.
ISBN-13: 978-0-531-20552-5 (lib. bdg.)   978-0-531-28101-7 (pbk.)
ISBN-10: 0-531-20552-5 (lib. bdg.)   0-531-28101-9 (pbk.)
1. Forest ecology—Juvenile literature. I. Title.
 QH541.5.F6B46 2011
 577.3—dc22   2010045933

All rights reserved. Published in 2011 by Children's Press, an imprint of Scholastic Inc.
Printed in China. 62
SCHOLASTIC, CHILDREN'S PRESS, A TRUE BOOK and associated logos are trademarks and/or registered trademarks of Scholastic Inc.

1 2 3 4 5 6 7 8 9 10 R 18 17 16 15 14 13 12 11

Find the Truth!

Everything you are about to read is true *except* for one of the sentences on this page.

Which one is **TRUE**?

T or F   Bears hibernate during the winter.

T or F   Cutting down trees can contribute to global warming.

Find the answers in this book.

3

Contents

THE BIG TRUTH!

Changing Colors

**Loggers from the
1890s**

Most temperate forest bats enter a deep sleep during winter months. ➡

A temperate forest in the fall

CHAPTER 1

Forest Features

Look at a world map. Find the lines of **latitude**. The lower latitudes are closer to the **equator**, which is at zero degrees. It is always warm in these areas.

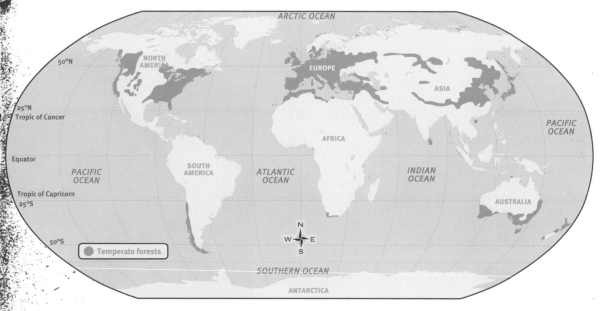

This map shows the major temperate forests on Earth.

Gray wolves help control
the populations of their prey
in temperate forests.

Upper latitudes are closer to the North and
South Poles, where it gets very cold. Temperate
forests are found between about 25 and 50
degrees latitude. This means they get a mixture
of different weather.

Weather in the Forest

Temperate forests get plenty of rain. This helps the forests' many plants to stay healthy. Some areas do not get as much rain as others. Temperate forests have different seasons. When it is summer and warm in the Northern **Hemisphere**, it is winter and cold in the Southern Hemisphere.

Temperate forests get between 30 and 60 inches (75 and 150 centimeters) of rain per year.

Leaves of deciduous trees usually turn orange, yellow, or bright red in the fall.

Deciduous Forests

There are two kinds of temperate forests. One is called the **deciduous** (de-SIJ-oo-uhss) forest. Deciduous trees have large, wide leaves to catch sunlight. Each year, these leaves change color and then fall off when the cold season arrives. This keeps the leaves from freezing, which could harm the trees. The trees' leaves start to grow back when the weather begins to get warm again.

Conifers, evergreen trees that produce seed-filled cones, have thin leaves called needles.

Evergreen Forests

The second kind of temperate forest is an evergreen forest. Evergreen trees do not shed their leaves like deciduous trees. One reason is that substances inside the leaves resist freezing. The leaves stay green all year. Some evergreen trees have wide leaves like deciduous trees. These trees are found in places where there is plenty of rain. Others have thin, hard leaves. They are found in drier areas.

Forest Layers

The top layer of a temperate forest is called a canopy. This layer is usually about 60 to 100 feet (20 to 30 meters) high. The next layer is called the subcanopy. It is made up of the tops of shorter trees. Below that is a layer of shrubs. Shrubs are shorter plants, such as bushes. The lowest layer is called ground cover. It is made up of grasses and mosses. Different animals live in each layer of the forest.

The world's tallest trees grow in temperate forests.

11

Squirrels depend on acorns from oak trees for part of their food.

CHAPTER 2

Forest Life

The temperate forest is filled with many different species of plants and animals. The plants, animals, and weather conditions in a certain area form an **ecosystem**. An ecosystem's species all depend on one another to survive. Plants get energy from the sun. They absorb food and water through the soil. Some animals eat the plants. Those animals are eaten by meat-eating animals.

There are about 450 different species of oak.

Types of Trees

Trees are a major part of temperate forest ecosystems. They provide shelter, oxygen, food, and water to many of a forest's other species. Oak, beech, maple, elm, and birch trees all grow in temperate forests. So do evergreen trees such as pines, firs, and spruces. Each kind of tree has leaves, bark, and branches that look different from other kinds.

The trunks of some trees, such as this spruce, are too broad to wrap your arms around.

Male elk, called bulls, grow a new set of antlers every year.

Elk often eat the grasses and wildflowers that grow on the forest floor.

More Forest Plants

Tall trees aren't the only plants found in temperate forests. The forest floor is covered with grasses. Some are short and green, like the grass in many people's yards. Others might be tall and stiff, like the bamboo found in Asian forests. Many different species of wildflowers add bright splashes of color to the forest. Shrubs and mosses are also commonly found in temperate forests.

An oak tree's roots can extend 50 feet (15 m) past the base of the tree.

Roots

Almost all temperate forest plants have roots that reach down into the soil. Plants use their roots to absorb water and nutrients from the soil. Large trees have huge roots that spread far underground. Smaller plants, such as grasses, have very short roots. The soil in temperate forests contains fungi that attach to tree roots. The fungi help the tree break down nutrients in the soil. In return, the fungi absorb nutrients from the roots.

Catching Some Sun

The leaves of plants contain a substance called **chlorophyll** (KLOR-uh-fill). Chlorophyll absorbs light energy from the sun. The plant then turns the light energy into energy the plant can use. This process is known as **photosynthesis** (foh-toh-SIN-thuh-siss). When the plant converts light energy, it absorbs carbon dioxide and gives off the oxygen that animals need to live. This means that photosynthesis is needed for almost all life on Earth.

Plant leaves are green because they contain chlorophyll.

Feeding the Animals

Plants provide food for many of the animals that live in temperate forests. Small animals, such as squirrels and birds, eat the seeds and nuts that fall to the forest floor. Deer, rabbits, and many other animals depend on leaves as a main part of their diets. Many plants also produce fruit, which attracts animals such as birds. Some animals even eat the bark that covers tree trunks.

White-tailed deer are common in North America's temperate forests.

Bears look for more than honey in a beehive. They also eat the bees living inside.

Meat Eaters

Temperate forests are also home to many meat-eating animal species. These species hunt other animals for food. Wolves work together to chase down deer. Bats snatch insects from the air as they fly at night. Snakes slither along the ground as they hunt for rats, mice, and other small animals. Some animals, such as bears, eat both plants and other animals.

As in most bird species, female cardinals are not as brightly colored as males.

Flying High

The temperate forest is home to birds of all sizes. Large birds, such as hawks and eagles, swoop down from the sky to catch mice and fish. Owls hunt at night. They hide in trees and wait for small animals to walk below them. Wild turkeys cannot fly long distances. They mostly eat seeds and insects. Temperate forests are also filled with smaller birds, such as robins, cardinals, and jays.

Worms and Insects

Worms and insects are as important to the temperate forest ecosystem as the other species that live there. Earthworms spend their lives burrowing underground. This keeps the soil loose and healthy so plants can grow. Bees carry pollen from flower to flower as they land to feed. This helps flowers make fruit or seeds. Insects and worms are also an important food source for many of the forest's larger animals.

Earthworms cannot see or hear, but they are able to sense light and movement.

CHAPTER 3

Hard Times

Winter is the hardest time of year for many of the temperate forest plants and animals. It gets very cold. Food is much harder to find. As the weather begins to change, the forest's wildlife begins preparing for the cold months. Each plant and animal species has its own way of surviving winter.

Red foxes listen for movement underground, and then dig through the snow and soil to locate their prey.

How Plants Prepare for Winter

Many plants in temperate forests shed their leaves before winter arrives. They must first prepare by growing special cells where the leaf attaches to the tree. Eventually, this layer of cells seals off the leaf from the branch. The leaf falls off. Many plants pull nutrients and minerals from the leaves before they fall off. These nutrients are stored in the tree's roots until the tree can start growing again.

A single maple tree loses 600,000 leaves every autumn.

Squirrels store nuts for winter, which they can recover when they need something to eat.

How Animals Prepare for Winter

During autumn, many animals begin growing thick hair all over their bodies. This winter coat will help keep them warm during the winter. The extra hair falls out once spring comes. This is called shedding. Many animals gather and store extra food while it is still easy to find. They can eat the extra food once their other food sources run out.

A hibernating animal's body temperature can drop below freezing. ➡️

Hibernating greater mouse-eared bats

Hibernation

Some animals **hibernate** to survive the harsh winter weather. Natural clues tell these creatures when the time is right to hibernate. For example, some animals start hibernating once the days become shorter and nights become longer.

Animals prepare for hibernation by eating lots of extra food. This gives them extra fat that their bodies can use for nutrients during the winter. Then they find warm hiding places and go into a deep sleep. Their body temperatures get very low. This helps them use less energy. Their heart rate and breathing rate drop, too.

Bears in Winter

For a long time, people thought that bears hibernated during the winter. We now know that this is not true. Bears become very slow during the winter. They spend almost all of their time sleeping. But unlike hibernating animals, bears' body temperatures do not drop. It is easy to wake one of these sleeping bears, but it is very difficult to wake a hibernating animal.

Bear cubs stay with their mothers during winter.

Torpor

Some animals only hibernate a little bit at a time. This is called **torpor**. Animals in torpor have lower body temperatures. But they only stay that way for a few hours at a time. Hibernating animals spend weeks at a time with low body temperatures. Certain bird species use torpor. So do some bats and mice.

Animals in torpor wake up each day or night to eat.

Pine marten

Birds often fly in a V formation when they migrate.

Migration

Some animals are able to avoid the cold winter weather. They do this by **migrating**. This means that they leave for warmer places when the weather gets cold. Once it warms up again, they return home. Many species of birds and fish migrate. So do some bats, insects, and mammals. Some animals travel thousands of miles every time they migrate.

Changing Colors

The leaves of deciduous trees turn beautiful colors in autumn. These brightly colored leaves look very different from the usual green ones. Leaves get their green coloring from the chlorophyll they use to capture light energy. As they get ready for winter, the trees stop making chlorophyll. This lets the other colors in the leaves show through.

The green coloring of chlorophyll is so strong that it covers up other colors in the leaf.

Yellow and orange colors have been in the leaves all along. But they are very light colors. This makes it easy for the green color to cover them up.

Trees start making red and purple colors in late summer. Even though they are dark colors, it is hard to see them until the green color disappears.

The weather in the spring, summer, and fall affect the timing and brightness of fall colors.

CHAPTER 4

Forests in Danger

Today, several factors threaten temperate forests. Many of these factors have to do with human activity. Logging is one of the biggest threats to temperate forests. Many logging companies cut down trees faster than they can grow back. This causes big problems for the forest ecosystem. Animals are left without homes, and there are not enough trees making oxygen.

Fast-growing softwoods, such as conifers, are often used in building houses.

Notebook paper, disposable towels, and toilet paper are made from trees.

Why Do People Cut Down Trees?

Many temperate forest trees are cut down for timber every year. People use the timber to make houses, furniture, and other items. The paper products we use every day are made from trees. Large areas of forest are often cut down to make room for farmland and mines.

Global Climate Change

Climate change is a shift in weather patterns. These changes affect temperatures, rainfall, and other factors. Global warming is a rise in world temperatures. Global warming causes climate change.

What do forests have to do with climate change? Animals breathe out a gas called carbon dioxide. Healthy trees use this gas as part of photosynthesis. They absorb the gas from the air and release oxygen which animals breathe in.

One of the largest factors in global warming is that vast areas have been cleared of trees.

Sometimes, people destroy forestland. They clear the trees to use the space for other purposes. The area might be used for farms or housing. Fewer trees are left to absorb carbon dioxide and make oxygen. Destroying trees also releases carbon dioxide into the air. Too much carbon dioxide in the **atmosphere** traps too much heat on Earth.

Hotter, drier climates also make it easier for wildfires to start. Wildfires can quickly destroy large amounts of forestland.

Wildfires burn millions of acres every year.

Power plants provide the electricity used in homes, schools, and businesses.

Pollution, Acid Rain, and Disease

Logging and wildfires aren't the only dangers that temperate forests face. Cars, factories, and power plants release harmful gases into the air. These gases mix with the water in the air and turn it into **acid rain**. This rain is bad for plants. It makes them unhealthy. They become too weak to fight off sicknesses such as chestnut blight or Dutch elm disease.

An ecosystem's plants, animals, and climate must be kept in balance for the ecosystem to be healthy.

CHAPTER 5

Conservation

The plants and animals of temperate forests cannot protect themselves from the dangers they face. Humans must find ways to prevent the damage or loss of these ecosystems. Without help, things will only get worse. Luckily, we can do some simple things to help keep the temperate forests healthy and alive.

Large populations of white-tailed deer can harm forests by eating trees before they can grow to full size.

Using Less Paper

One easy way to help preserve temperate forests is to buy fewer paper products. Use washable cloth napkins instead of paper ones. Bring reusable bags when you go to the grocery store. Avoid printing paper copies from your computer unless you really need them. When you do use paper products, don't throw them in the trash. Recycling them instead will help save our forests.

Recycling is an easy way to save paper.

Timeline: The History of Paper

105 C.E.
Paper is invented in China.

1450
The printing press is invented, increasing demand for paper.

More Ways to Help

Cars are one of the biggest causes of air pollution. Avoid riding in cars when you take short trips. Instead, try walking or riding a bike. You can also help preserve temperate forests by planting trees and other plants in your neighborhood. This can help to balance out the trees that are cut down by logging companies, miners, and farmers.

1690

The first U.S. paper mill is built in Philadelphia by Benjamin Franklin.

late 1800s

Papermakers begin using wood instead of linen to make paper.

2008

People in the United States throw out 77.4 million tons of paper.

Spreading the Word

Temperate forests are beautiful and important ecosystems. They are home to thousands of species of plants and animals. But many people do not know about the problems facing these forests. It is important that we spread information about them to as many people as we can. If we work hard, we can make sure temperate forests will last for many years to come. ★

Each year, the U.S. forest industry plants 10 trees for every person in the country.

Planting trees is one way people try to help save forests.

The oldest living thing on Earth: A 4,700-year-old bristlecone pine tree in Nevada.

Amount of forestland in the United States: 747 million acres (302.5 million hectares)

Area planted with trees each year by forest landowners in the United States: 2.5 million acres (1 million ha)

Amount of paper each U.S. citizen uses each year: Approximately 700 pounds (300 kg)

South American forestland lost each year: About 10 million acres (4 million ha)

African forestland lost each year: About 8.4 million acres (3.4 million ha)

Number of U.S. wildfires in 2009: 78,792

Amount of landfill space taken up by paper: 25 percent

Did you find the truth?

(F) Bears hibernate during the winter.

(T) Cutting down trees can contribute to global warming.

Resources

Books

Champion, Neil. *Temperate Woodlands*. North Mankato, MN: Smart Apple Media, 2007.

Serafini, Frank. *Looking Closely Through the Forest*. Toronto: Kids Can Press, 2008.

Tagliaferro, Linda. *Explore the Deciduous Forest*. Mankato, MN: Capstone Press, 2007.

Trammel, Howard K. *Wildfires*. New York: Children's Press, 2009.

Wojahn, Rebecca Hogue, and Donald Wojahn. *A Temperate Forest Food Chain: A Who-Eats-What Adventure in North America*. Minneapolis: Lerner Publications, 2009.

Woodward, John. *Temperate Forests*. Chicago: Raintree, 2011.

Organizations and Web Sites

Kids Do Ecology: World Biomes: Temperate Forest
http:// kids.nceas.ucsb.edu/biomes/temperateforest.html
Learn more about the plants and animals that live in temperate forests.

Maine Foliage: Kids' Page: General Tree and Forest Facts
www.maine.gov/doc/foliage/kids/forestfacts.html
Read some fun facts about trees.

Our Forests & Parks: Where the Other You Lives
www.discovertheforest.org/?r=thevid
Look at pictures and find forests near you.

Places to Visit

Green Mountain National Forest
231 North Main Street
Rutland, VT 05701
(802) 747-6700
www.fs.fed.us/r9/forests/
greenmountain/htm/
greenmountain/g_home.htm
Take a hike and enjoy the colorful trees of this huge forest.

Prince William Forest Park
18100 Park Headquarters Road
Triangle, VA 22172-1644
(703) 221-7181
www.nps.gov/prwi/
Camp out in a 15,000-acre (6,000 ha) temperate forest.

Important Words

acid rain (ASS-id RAYN)—rain that is polluted by harmful gases in the air

atmosphere (AT-muhss-fihr)—gases around a planet

chlorophyll (KLOR-uh-fill)—the green substance in plants that absorbs light energy

deciduous (de-SIJ-oo-uhss)—describing plants that shed their leaves every year

ecosystem (EE-koh-siss-tuhm)—a community of plants and animals and the environment they live in

equator (i-KWAY-tur)—an imaginary line around the middle of the Earth

hemisphere (HEM-uhss-fihr)—one-half of Earth

hibernate (HYE-bur-nate)—to go into a deep winter sleep where body temperature drops very low

latitude (LAT-uh-tood)—a measurement of how far a place is from the equator

migrating (MYE-grate-ing)—moving to a warmer place during the winter

photosynthesis (foh-toh-SIN-thuh-siss)—the process of using chlorophyll to capture light energy and turn it into food

torpor (TOR-pur)—a state of lower body temperature that allows an animal to use less energy

Index

Page numbers in **bold** indicate illustrations

About the Author

Peter Benoit is educated as a mathematician but has many other interests. He has taught and tutored high school and college students for many years, mostly in math and science. He also runs summer workshops for writers and students of literature. Mr. Benoit has also written more than 2,000 poems. His life has been one committed to learning. He lives in Greenwich, New York.